The Tiger Side of Night

The Tiger Side of Night

for Barb, who is

Olga Costopoulos

One Very Strong Tiger,

With Admiration,

Olga

Ekstasis Editions

Library and Archives Canada Cataloguing in Publication

Costopoulos, Olga

   The Tiger Side of Night / Olga Costopoulos

   Poems.

ISBN 1-894800-73-7

   I. Title.

PS8613.A4597P37 2006   C811'.6   C2006-906621-0

© 2006 Olga Costopoulos
Cover art: Hildegard von Bingen
Author Photo: Bert Almon

Published in 2006 by:
Ekstasis Editions Canada Ltd.
Box 8474, Main Postal Outlet
Victoria, B.C. V8W 3S1

Ekstasis Editions
Box 571
Banff, Alberta T0L 0C0

The Canada Council for the Arts | Le Conseil des Arts du Canada
Since 1957 | Depuis 1957

British Columbia Arts Council
Supported by the Province of British Columbia

The Tiger Side of Night has been published with the assistance of grants from the Canada Council for the Arts and the British Columbia Arts Council administered by the Cultural Services of British Columbia. The author would like to acknowledge the assistance of the Alberta Foundation for the Arts for the completion of this manuscript.

This book is for Bert, Meli, and Vasilis and Tatiana, and friends everywhere.

Contents

I. Now You, Too, Must Remember

Hand Poems	13
White Magpie	19
Astronomy Lessons	21
A Wild Tiger Lily	22
An Improbability of Cranes	25
Sketch of the Old Man	26
Life Beside the Battle	27
Deconsecrations	31
Waterwitch	33
Lampblack	34
Roamin' in the Gloamin'	35
Balance of Nature	36
Apocalypse, Then?	37
Animal Fairy Stories	38
Tarpits	40
Silent Thunder	41

II. A Little World Made Cunningly

Believe Me When I Tell You of the Mallow Plant	45
A Little World Made Cunningly	46
Only Women Born in May	47
On Being Asked to Contribute Poetry to a Time Capsule	49
Ginkgo	50
A Meditation on Sleep	51
Feel Your Way	52
Text/Con/Text	53
To the Lady Next Door	54
Hardhat	55
Gesundheit	57
On Finding Yet Another Fineliner Pen…	59
For I Shall Consider My Beloved	61
Moons	62
The Lucky Ones	65

Binaries	66
"The Most Recent 5000 Years of Chinese Art"	67
Mosaic Tiles, Bathing Room, Fishbourne	73
"Ovid's Love Nest Found By Banks of the Tiber"	74
Elgin Marbles, British Museum	75
Docent Muse	76

III. THE TIGER SIDE OF THE NIGHT

Icons	81
Cleopatra: The Final Sting	87
Ironing	88
Cleaning Windows	89
Blue and White	90
The Comfort of Lists	91
Laryngitis	92
Radius	94
Failing the Eye Exam	95
Bone Scan	96
Breaking Through	97
The Widower	98
Sub-Titled	99
The Tiger Side of the Night	100
For Dodie	101
Stones	102
Hampstead	107
Red Rose, White Rose	111
Balancing Act	112
Fugue State	113
What You Will Need	114
Pazyryk Fragment	115

The Tiger Side of Night

I
Now You, Too, Must Remember

Hand Poems

> *God lives in the details.*
> Aby Warburg

I Ancestral Hands

All ancestral photographs look alike.

They lie in stern and sepia silence
clasping each other in a sable lap
or resting, lightly,
on the bearded patriarch's shoulder.
The faces of wife and daughter
are indistinguishable, one wed
too young, to sorrow, one born,
too soon, to the same.
Both wear the same high-collared darks,
the same grave mouths seem closed from habit,
the same knowledge troubles their gaze,
a counter-accusation of the camera.
The only difference is in the hands:
the ringed fingers are clenched,
the unringed poised for flight.

II Hired Hands

Another old photograph with names
written in a pointed European hand:
"Harry und Frieda Friedman und kinder, 1919."
They stand surrounded
by their ten scrubbed children.
All hands are joined, the faces serious
but the pose is hopeful.

I return to this picture often
just to hear my father repeat their story:
Frieda gave birth in the night
then went out at dawn to milk the cows
to get milk for the breakfast porridge.
My grandfather had to order her back to bed.
The photo reveals twelve lives
reduced to two "hired hands."

III The Cook's Hands

They never took a picture of Mrs. Leitau
whose story was always prompted by the Friedmans'.
I was named after her.
A widow from somewhere back east
she'd come with her small daughter
to cook on my grandfather's ranch.
She soon became a local legend—
roasts so tender you didn't need a knife,
butter so sweet you could do without honey,
bread—who needed pie for dessert?

Her kindness was also legendary:
My father remembered her nursing him
through the 'flu of 1918
with hot broth and cold sponge baths.
At ninety-three he still recalled
how cool her hands felt,
how he knew he was safe with her.

I imagine her in the ranch kitchen
rolling pastry with those cool strong hands
still stained from the saskatoons
picked in the early morning
or out in the yard at soapmaking
standing over the vat, hands red with lye.
Mrs. Leitau, who were you?
Where did you fly to when Grandma arrived
in a later wagon, with her pressed glass,
her pursed lips, and her suspicion?

IV My Father's Hands

Those were the hands that terrified in their hugeness.
Fingers that could reach clear around my childish trunk,
my adult upper arms.
We watched him, at 76, grasp the horns of a bull
and flip the beast onto the ground, with no more than a
"Sonovabitch." Without fear, without, even, outrage.

He clipped all his nails with hoof-trimmers,
the only instrument fit for the job.
I remember the click of those nails on the ivory
buttons of the small accordion he called "the donkey guts."
He emended tunes to suit himself.
Except The Missouri Waltz.

At 93, liver-spotted skin
drapes over the still-huge bones.
The pulse wavers in the protean web
between thumb and forefinger.
The hands clutch at nothing, at everything
in morphine-directed chores.
Sitting with him in his hospital room,
offering him a paper cup of water,
I come to these last futile acts
with no more understanding
than when he perhaps offered me
my first water from my own first cup.
All I can think of is how like the cave bear
skeleton in the Rock Shop in Drumheller
are his hands. Try to remember which period
of pre-history they've both come from.

V My Sister's Hands

Too large, they said, for a woman
so they made her do men's work.
The hands learned the hard balance
of downward force on the plough handles
against the forward urging of the mule.
She learned the coordination of squeeze
and pull, her head buried, along with her dreams,
in the warm flank of the cow,
while the milk frothed in the bucket.
So skilled she could squirt the wild barn cats.
Learned how to reach into that other womb
to turn the calf about to breach
while singing a midwife's lullaby
to the terrified cow.
Hard lessons of maternity.

Now they fold into each other, blue-veined, pale,
in repose so still they startle.
The fingernails form natural Gothic arches,
with perfect oval moons rising at their bases.

She wished for music
bought herself a grand piano
with money saved from the housekeeping.
But it was too late: the rhythm of the plough
the milk pail and cow's tail conspired,
thrust their own awkward measures upon her,
her fingers could never master
a lightsome prestissimo.
She walks undaunted, andante, across the fields
carrying with just enough grace the wild pinks
she's rescued from the combine's path.

VI My Hands

The pair of them, they're conspiring against me
with their budgie-beak fingernails
that click code to each other,
defying the manicurist's clippers.
Their perversely pointed fingers
have never been quite right
for either piano keys or 'cello neck.
And now they won't even work together,
Sinistra claiming arthritis in the thumb joints,
Dexter still showing off, trilling, crowing.

And both of them—swelling up
like the Michelin man—or worse,
the Pillsbury doughboy,
just when I want to wear a ring.
Their backs are wrinkled with blue veins
that stand out like mountain ranges
rising out of a desert on a satellite photo.
All the emollients of Switzerland
will not soften these great paws.

I shouldn't resent their gracelessness.
They caress, make decent bread,
wash floors to immaculacy,
and would strangle with ease
anyone who would threaten harm
to my beloved or my children.

White Magpie

Work-morning, parking lot,
our first sighting of a new species—
a magpie in shape, but white, white as gull-breast,
pale grey wings stolen from a dove
and slightly darker tail. Not an albino.
The feathered anomaly moves a few magpie paces off,
a proverb in action, whose wings will remain
fluttering against the edges of the mind.

September 29th, my mother's birthday,
another dream of her—I'm carrying her—
she is almost weightless—
into a house for shelter,
or out of a house that's burning.
I always awake distraught, having to remind myself
she's been gone these eleven years
and I couldn't save her then, either.

She was small, bird-like toward the end.
With no more malice than manners,
a small boy once called her "an old crow"
despite her waves of pure white hair.
Her own granddaughter, nicknamed "Sugarplum,"
named her "Granny Sugarprune."

The bird steps closer again
looks at me with one gold, knowing eye
then, as in a dream, opens its beak
to explain itself, but I hear no sound
through the closed window.
The golden eye keeps watching me.
I keep hearing the gold claws
on the tiled floor of my dreams.

How like her quiet humour
to come as this ruffian fowl
but wearing the colours of the dove.

Astronomy Lesson

Two things fill the mind with ever-increasing wonder and awe: the starry heavens above me, and the moral law within me.
                        Immanuel Kant

The crocuses that purpled the hill
had silvered in the moonlight the evening
my sister led me up to the top behind our house
to introduce me to the stars.
She spread blankets and a map of the skies
shone a flashlight on the paper
pointed out the patterns
then switched off
the light.
We lay on our backs
and she told me stories
about all the constellations—
the word wheeled in my head
rolled off my tongue and just
when I thought I had tamed Ursa Major,
found the Pole Star at the zenith, Orion's belt
and the Pleiades, she told me about infinity.
The word seemed to echo outward
towards its own meaning, and I, weightless,
heaven and earth ranging around me,
reached over the edge of my blanket,
grabbed a crocus with each hand
as close to the root as possible,
and clung to the earth
dizzy from
flight.

A Wild Tiger Lily

I STONE CIRCLES

That pasture: first lesson in geometry—
stone circles, tipi rings, all broken precisely
in the middle of their southeast quadrants
to face away from prevailing winds.
An untaught lesson in geology—
so many stones, so many shapes, sizes,
a United Melting Glacial Nations
or remains of giants' children having rockfights—
so many colors, such surprising hefts—
the feathery salt-taffy pumice
blocks of salt-lick decoy red sandstone
the gravitas of granite.
Limestone caught and held the noon sun
to give back glow and warmth at sunset.
I, proud owner of a rock cow ranch,
made up stories about them all.

Beyond a hill, off to the east,
was a chair-sized stone, so big
no one could ever have moved it—
someone else's thinking stone too?
The pasture's been strip-mined, its contours gone—
replaced by mountains of uniform grey
clay so slick when it rains nothing can stand—
and everything slides to the bottom,
to drown in the giant's footprints.

II THE SPRING

The summer a mouse got into the well
and my mother became hysterical—
the only time in her life—
we had to get water from the spring
until a new well could be drilled.

I was allowed to walk the half-mile there
and even carry my own small bucket
to this place mysterious, dangerous,
compelling as an unexpected smile.
Here the water emerged from its lush grass
chuckling at a secret joke told by a gnome
from deep in the earth, below the horse-trail
we rode each unmysterious day.

The days were hot, but the water, so cold
as it rilled over hands, onto stones
and on down the hillside
to disappear into the willowed creek.

My father dug out a small reservoir
and sank a metal cylinder into it
to give the water a place to clarify itself
collect, and await the dipping bucket.
He could always put a stop to laughter.

III The Other Spring

This one was closer to home
but was pronounced "alkali."
We were always warned away from it,
but I made the forbidden visit often
to see what new things had surfaced
and eventually worked their way out
from muddy centre toward dry ground.

This water rose up from the earth silent,
clear, slow, filling the spongy hoof prints
pressed by indolent cattle who'd drink
from the muddy bowls they'd made.

A wild tiger lily grew near that spring.
Alone in that inhospitable ground
defiant in the breeze, saying
"I've learned to survive on my own here.
I dare you brute beasts to try and eat me."
For reasons of their own, the cows weren't biting.

An Improbability of Cranes

They appeared in an Easter sky just before sunset
I was first to hear them, and heard before I saw them.
Their sound was a tuneless yodeling
The sun sent red-gold notes from their wings
The line became a cluster, then landed—
a ceremonious coming-to-ground in the ploughed field.
Migration had thinned them, body and number.

Their grace on land is an awkward one—slow,
a mincing walk that says "this ground simply will not do"
or the mono-footed stance that tempts kids
to sneak up behind and push them over.
Necks just begging to be wrung
for such unmusical earthbound conversation.
Red throat-feathers appear, on close inspection,
to have run into the adjacent white.
Inedible. Ungainly fowl.

Over summer I forgot that northward flight,
concerned with my own awkwardness.

Autumn afternoon: digging spuds, mudbound
clumsy in caked Wellingtons that belong
to the sibling two sizes larger than me.
Then that yodeling cry sounds from a far hill,
and the long line of notes appears
black against the red-gold sunset.
I throw down my spade to stand
ridiculous and dumb in the presence of such glory.

Sketch of the Old Man

He walks slowly, proud as a pregnant woman,
his huge hands spread to span
the "bellyful of gallstones they finally found."

Like the sloth, he should be easy to catch
in body, or at least in the eye of the mind.
But there is no cage big enough,

and the mind's eye is too small a screen:
he fills it as he filled and darkened
the doorways of my childhood.

When my brother, looking up from the paper,
asked, "What is rape, Dad?" he answered:
"Breedin' a woman against her will."

When my mother, fetching coal,
broke her knee falling down the cellar steps,
he said, "A horse a man could shoot."

To me, at the end of high school:
"Get more schooling. With a face like yours
you'll never find a man to keep you."

To me, on the death of my first husband:
"If ya hafta marry agin, don't marry an Englishman."
(This in my English mother's presence)

To my mother, about my daughter:
"Ain't she a pleasant thought."
She avoids him when he visits.

I still read *King Lear*, but cannot teach it.

Life Beside the Battle

    I

Every crossing of the Battle River revives their story—
a log house, their first, on the south bank of the river
but well above the flood plain
a constant worry of my father's.
He didn't seem to mind the snow blowing in
between the badly chinked logs.
My sister remembers that once,
she and our brother watched a weasel wriggle in
through a hole, seeking shelter.
He left quickly, disappointed.

II

For a man who hated rivers, he talked a lot
about the Missouri, the Mississippi.
He'd crossed both on his way to Canada.
He settled so near the river, but never
allowed his children within a hundred yards of it.
The neighbor kids could all swim like otters
before they were five. He claimed they were
failed drownings.

III

We cross the Battle upstream from the home place.
Same old bridge, but here the stream is calm.
I let my gaze leave the black asphalt river
flowing smooth beneath us,
slide over the great valley we're in,
let the strata of its deep walls remind me
how quickly his ninety-three years passed.

His body in the plain pine box he chose
lies beyond pain or accusation.
The nose once straight, perfect,
has begun its subsidence, inexorable
as I once thought him.

IV

As per request, "no funeral, no church."
So I stand with my husband, son, and sister,
in the south-west corner of the cemetery,
apart from the pack of male descendants
all eager for a look at the will and a smoke.
It's warm for October, but I feel the chill.

The cowboy preacher fumbles for words,
pretending there was a deathbed conversion.
I want to deny it, but keep silent.
Then a sudden barking turns our heads
neither hounds of hell nor coyotes,
just a great river of gold in the sky—
Snow geese flying west, in V after rippling V,
the morning sun dazzling from beneath their wings.

Deconsecrations

The prairie wool lies deep, uncut for years.
No farmer wants to risk a mower blade
or a charge of disrespect to the dead
beneath the toppled headstones.
The rock and key beneath it are still easy to find.
Inside we see no need for locks.
The reed organ I'd played my first hymns on
was stolen some time in the sixties
by thieves who knew what they'd come for.
A lovely baroque instrument,
already an antique when purchased—
finely carved woods and ivory-faced stops—
the parish farmers had sent for it
to their home village in France

The scents of candles and incense are gone
replaced by mouse-must, pigeon droppings, death.
I am warned about hanta virus, but
feel that this place once so sacred
must hold some residual protection.
The simple fleur-de-lis altar carvings
are intact, but the built-in reliquary door
hangs open, half-unhinged, revealing
the decomposing carcass of a pigeon.

Old habit flexes the knee
on the way to the curtained confessional.
The burgundy brocade has rotted into tatters,
and now I see with older eyes a corner
so small, so close to the front pew
that the priest was likely not the only one
who heard confessions before Sunday mass.

The church was deconsecrated in 1964,
and though I now know more of doubt than faith
something in me wants to stop these ravages,
repair the windows, rehinge the reliquary,
restore the altar, give that pigeon
a decent burial beneath the prairie wool,
clean house for the dove of the Holy Spirit,
find, return, retune that small sweet organ.

I've placed the wooden signboard on my wall:
Notre Dame de Savoie, 1910 - 1964
It's there for safekeeping
until reconsecration.
I'm not sure whose,
I'm not sure when.

Waterwitch

He used to divine wells for other farmers,
only he called it witching for water.
They trusted him because he doubted.
The Catholic neighbors, all churchgoers,
agreed it was all right to do something
as long as nobody believed in it.
Their disbelief was their charm
against the chthonian magic,
even as they carried water in buckets
from the witched well to the baptismal font.

Lampblack

I sit near the back, hoping for sleep
but the night outside the bus is so dark
it keeps me wide-eyed, hungry for light.
We're still close enough to the city
to see commercial greenhouses—
bricks of a distant radiance
or soft pats of butter melting
into the black bread of the landscape.

The night completes its blackening chores
leaving only an occasional gleam
of anonymous yellow eyes.

My mother's game comes back to me now—
after we'd polished the thin glass chimneys
of the squat coal oil lamps
it was my job to shake the rags outdoors.
"Shake hard," she'd say, "so the wind can carry
the black to where night is needed.
Corn grows in the night."
Nothing so benign, so golden
as corn grew in my nights.

I shook with such conviction
as would rid the world of night,
send the blacking packing
to someplace behind the stars.

Roamin' in the Gloamin'

Scratched out by a dull needle
on the strange-smelling black disk,
the singer sounded old like his words—
"Roamin' in the gloamin'
On the bonny banks o' Clyde—"

The words and the swingeing violin
conjured a tense purple landscape
although I knew nothing of heather.

"Roamin' in the gloamin'
wi' me lassie by me side—"

Did the singer mean that long-nosed Collie?

"When the sun has gone to rest
That's the time tha' I like best—"

The purple deepened
along with my confusion and my
fascination with the full glottal stop.

"Oh i's lovely roamin' in the gloamin'."

Now, of an evening, though the whisky is golden
I look for the gloaming in my glass.

Balance of Nature

Up north, she keeps a true bush garden—
that is, a garden true to the bush.
No pampered European transplants here,
just wild things, invited in, encouraged.
Here lady's slippers grow by shooting stars
both nodded over by wild lupine, saskatoon.
She's poached them all from forest reserves
of the multi-national Paper-Corp.

Her son programs the company's computers
for maximum efficiency of the plant
where the forest is devoured, digested
and homogenized into newsprint, diapers,
and computer paper.

Will she have time to fill her floral ark
before he programs the last log
into the hopper, before
a new dictionary is printed
with new words like feller-buncher,
delimber, and skiddragger, without
lady's slipper, without shooting star?

Apocalypse, Then?

Three when the dream first came:

standing at the open east window of the farmhouse
Very real.
leaning forearms on the windowsill
conscious of my waist being at the same height
knowing dream because the real windowsill
is at least to my chest in the daytime.
Waist is a border between
the two warring halves of me.
I wait in a thick, eye-straining dark.
The dawn begins orange across the valley
black is purpling at the edges of my breathing
and four helmeted knights on pale grey horses
ride into the farmyard, three of them stopping
at my window, so close I can smell the horses.
All heads are level: horses, men, mine.
The fourth, whose horse is dappled,
rides on around the corner,
looks in at another window,
sees that my window
is only the top half
of a Dutch door.
He laughs,
the door
falls open
I fall
awakening
just before
the rearing horses'
hooves strike home.

Animal Fairy Stories

At three, I found it a very large book
had to climb into a chair to make enough lap for it.
It must have been new when it came to me—
I still remember the new-book smell.
The cover was hard, bright, shiny.
There bunnies frolicked fat and laughing
on a flowery green meadow,
holding paws in a raucous round dance.
They were not the lean brown jackrabbits
that dodged prickly pear in pastures I knew.
Inside, the pictures were so softly drawn
even the wolves looked friendly.
I tried to pet them into life.
What's more, they could talk, and did—
speaking more in one short story
than my two-legged pack uttered in a day.

The word "fairy," my sister explained,
meant "a small, imaginary winged creature."
(I knew it was special because she didn't call it a "critter.")
To me it meant a secret world of moonlit gardens, ponds, and music.
"But nobody really believes in fairies, and you mustn't, either."
I already had my sense of the forbidden,
and pondered in private why nobody believed
what I knew to be true.
It seemed my father was right:
"Believe none of what you hear
and about half of what you see."

I was the youngest child, the only reader, so
I guess it was I who wore the book out—
The last time I saw it, on a visit home,
it was coverless, tattered, with dirty threads
hanging from its naked, broken spine.
I couldn't resist a quick, surreptitious read-through,
this time recognizing Aesop, the Brothers Grimm
this time able to separate the charmed world
where small creatures learned big lessons
and none came to lasting harm
from the real world, where truth remains
elusive as the small white rabbits of memory.

Tarpits

> *I'm afraid that if my demons leave me, my angels will desert me too.*
> Rainer Maria Rilke

The needles are losing their efficacy.
The doctor has suggested hypnosis
"to free the ch'i blocked by childhood trauma."
Can those tar pits ever be siphoned out?

And could the attendant demons then
collect employment insurance?
Or would they just dig new depressions?
Might angels then come trooping in
to clean the place, earn their keep
fending off the demons?

Or, if it were that easy, could one say,
sotto voce, "Magic Time," pass a hand
in front of the face and carry on
like an actor, knowing precisely
where the lights are, but acknowledging
only what lies beyond them?

Silent Thunder

The first attack
was like the first lightning of summer—
hard to believe in its suddenness and silence—
no time to scream
the knife was as silent as the lightning that gashed the sky
she expected some grownup to hear,
to respond in thunderous rage—
she counted a long time
but blood is silent even when it surges
from the deep arteries between
the wounding and the pain.
No one awakened in the darkened house.
And still the scar hushes her among candles.
She's listening to the outraged blood
that boils up through the years of silence
to thunder inside her carefully poised head.

II
A Little World Made Cunningly

Believe Me When I Tell You of the Mallow Plant

I have proof.
There is a large backlit picture of one
at the local Botanical Garden.
Single, a bright orange-red
with a small, bright yellow centre.
Foliage: silver-grey; Growth: no more
than fifteen centimetres tall,
and only in soil recently disturbed.

I found them growing in the gumbo ruts
left by the trucks of the oil company
that sank a well in my father's land.
I didn't go into the pasture
the summer the rig was there.
My mother told me not to.
After the drillers all left, I went,
picked every one of the flowers.
She hadn't told me not to.

She couldn't identify the plant,
could recollect no disturbance
of soil in her childhood in England.

The flower that grew from the coarse rut is gone,
its red-orange glow extinguished.
But I remember.
And now I have told you.

A Little World Made Cunningly

Against the brown fence
racemes of white bleeding hearts
bloom like rows of postulants
awaiting communion
quiver at bee and breeze alike
refusing the black and yellow workers
admission to their scentless convexities

Against the same brown fence
a mossed wire basket hangs—
as near as I've come to Babylon—
from its bower of trailing rosemary
a deep scarlet begonia promises
darker, deeper, softer things, its petals
flaring like a Spanish dancer's skirts

Between the white and the scarlet
a Jacob's Ladder rises, a rectitude
of multilateral kaleidoscopic symmetry
crowned by a host of modest purple blossoms.
Listen: can you hear the angel panting?

Only Women Born in May

I Lily of the Valley

It has nothing to do with superstition.
These are rules my mother taught
to replace another catechism.
Only women born in May can wear emeralds,
wear Lily-of-the-Valley perfume.
Only witches grow black flowers.
Red carnations are only suitable
to celebrate worldly success.
Tradescantia sends esteem, but not love.
Violets praise, and ought to raise a modest blush.
Gardenias are sent to women loved in secret.

II Virgin's Bower

Yellow roses from a man to a woman
are a sure curse.
I knew my friend's marriage was doomed
not because he was a classically-trained musician
and she was a stewardess:
in a stupid attempt to impress her
with his knowledge of a popular song
he courted her with 18 yellow roses.

I didn't know the English name
of the clematis vines I planted
outside my living room window
to cover a dull brown wall.
Had no idea that it would bring you
like a bee to borage
to claim the place prepared for you
on my sofa—a place where you can stretch out
contemplate the white and purple glory
which whispers, over my shoulder,
"I love your mind as well."

On Being Asked to Contribute Poetry To a Time Capsule Which Is To Be Buried in the Foundation of the New Concert Hall

"What will survive of us is love."
          Philip Larkin

Only the ephemeral is forever;
the only thing permanent is your gesture

A friend asks me, "How do you do it?
How is it you two are still in love
after all these years?" (It's only been twenty.)
I tell her, 'Blind Luck. He's blind
to my flaws, and I'm lucky."
But if I can't explain to the present,
what shall I tell the future?
Is it that we'd shared so much of life
before we even met that it seemed
we'd always been waiting for each other?
When you hear this, we will be there,
hovering, hand in ghostly hand, above
a hundred-year-old concert hall
where we will have sat, hand in warm hand
and thrilled to Dvorak's Cello Concerto.

And what do I leave to posterity?
Only what it chooses to confer upon me.
My trust is in my beloved's eyes
my hope is in my children's laughter
my belief, as I sleep in the stone,
is in the power of the music.
We may not be allowed the luxury
of dying in each other's arms.
I am consoled that with these words
we will be resurrected together.

Ginkgo

For My Daughter

Plant seeds in clay, not plastic,
first partially chipping off the hard coats
the seeds that look like nuts—so hard
dark brown, almost invulnerable
only a little softer inside
they could travel the world for decades
without losing that tough shell
or the procreative energy locked within.
(I understand why you wore your coat
for all three years of high school.)

They rest in a cool dark cupboard.
You store your sweet perfumes there
beside these germs of the foulest-smelling tree
(they also keep better in cool darkness)
scents that will one day unlock
urges powerful as trees' to sun.

I don't check the pots very often—
gardeners learn patience
to let mystery happen.
And while I covertly watch you
as you watch World Cup soccer
I know I will not see the germination
when eye meets eye to set
another generation into motion.

A Meditation on Sleep

Dreamwebs still shadowing my eyes
I see it on the shelf beside the bed
its two black straps still curved parentheses
a mutilated spinner, two-legged now,
it has toiled so long
the other six have staggered off—
Or maybe it's a different pest that's been
masticating the tender minutes
of the green-leaf blanket I call sleep—
I suspect a praying mantis.
But it could also be
that the mammoth of my dreamtime is grazing
in the oldest pastures of my slumber,
sharing the truffles of remembered pleasures
he lifts with his tusks so tenderly
neither they nor the dreams are punctured.
One day, I will awaken free from pain,
discover in my hand a hair—
coarse, long, auburn,
a souvenir from the mammoth's forelock.
I shall fashion it into a new watchband.

Feel Your Way

Searching the room for any lost object
everything looks too familiar
in its usual out-of-place spot—
the books ranged almost alphabetically,
the pictures in front of the books, aslant
away from the sun's wintry weakness
athwart the moonbeams that define the blinds

You might sometime search in total darkness
seek with your hands and come to know this room
new again, unsensed before by touch—
the smooth birch dresser, the matte-finish pot
that holds the fat-leafed jade tree
the smooth curved face of a porcelain clock
the fine weave of a small handled basket
a textured slope of a linen lampshade
the rough stone I picked up at Towton Field.

Your fingers would assume a writing stance
on my keyboard. You could type a message
for my later finding.
Your palms could caress the outreaching leaves
of the two bedside African violets.
Now a familiar perfume beckons

let yourself be found, embraced—at last—
by warmth you know
beyond every sense.

Text/Con/Text

The tallest young man in my freshman class
politely sits at the back of the room.
He tells me he plays hockey. Professionally.
Perhaps he wonders why I blush at this.
Should I confess that I once smiled and said
a warm "Hello, how are you?" to Gretzky
all the while searching my mental file drawer
of class lists past, not finding it.
Where did he sit? What year?
Did he pass?
I strode away in consternation
at my failing memory, then knocked down
the life-size cutout of the unremembered
as I tripped on the very real stick he'd just signed.
I apologized to the effigy, then realized
I was probably the only person in this town
to practise such iconoclasm
with no more penalty than the sweet smile
he'd given me as he said, "Fine, thank you."

The third week of classes, I'm out shopping
when my hockey-playing student shoots
around the end of the feminine hygiene aisle.
Once again, I smile and say "Hello,"
this time confident of both names.
Tongue-tied, he stares at me and my cart
as if my bagels were hockey pucks,
my celery a bundle of hockey sticks.
He can only stammer and flee.
They think we all sleep in drawers
in our office filing cabinets,
or materialize out of the text
just prior to each class.

To the Lady Next Door

Don't tell me that the hedgehog I fed has fleas;
are you certified free of parasites?
The sparrow I buried in the garden was a lousy nuisance?
The jackrabbit has a foul temper when cornered?
(I've seen enough of yours when you've got your own space.)

Don't complain to me about the groundhog
that ate your green beans and left only the wax ones
you don't particularly like (but your husband does).

If you didn't want the great blue heron
to eat up all the goldfish in your water garden
maybe you should have shared your smelts with him.

And if you can't stand the swallow-shit on your porch
then kill your own damn mosquitoes.

Hardhat

Construction cranes everywhere
and their slow dances mesmerize.
I forget my driving, watching
the carefully awkward cable
swing a girder into place
imagining the steel made rigid
as much by fear as tungsten
that this fragile bough may break, let fall
its burden before it can be placed—
with what could be mistaken
for a stiff tenderness—
into its three-dimensional puzzle.

The man appears at a different site each day
in hardhat and goggles: he must be a site inspector
or at very least, a foreman, overseeing everything.
His whole upper body moves
with every twist and swing of the crane.
He directs his steel ballet like von Karajan—
a wide arching motion with his whole arm,
closing his eyes at the most intense moments—
when the girder slips into its slot—
then presses his hands together
in thanks, or silent satisfaction.
Then the real foreman walks over to him,
turns his wheelchair around
and points the way off the site.

When I worked in a medical library
I was issued a lab-coat.
The nearest I came to clinical work
was taking a phone message to a surgeon:
his research dog had died.

The hardhat circumscribes nothing
but the minds outside it.
Why is it that those who work
with their minds wear only clothes
but those who work with their bodies
protect mainly their heads?

Gesundheit

I On The Record

The first sound on the DECCA FFR recording
of Sir Georg Solti directing Parzifal
live from the Festspielhaus in Bayreuth
is a sneeze.
Not some strictly composed, fully rehearsed,
nicely suspended cadential orchestral sneeze
à la Hary Janos. No. This is a
caught-the-victim-completely-off-his-guard
90-decibel eruption sending 200-miles-per-hour
spittle, shock waves and shudders
through this lofty Teutonic hall.
The audience here knows that a sneeze
before any utterance negates what follows
like a retraction before the first note.
Was it the ghost of Nietzsche?

II Off the Record

Your sneezes always catch you out,
convulse you, leave you discomposed,
pockets turned out, but your hands
still searching, too late, for a handkerchief.
I've quit checking the cupboard
to make sure the crystal is still intact
while you stand, beggared by your own body,
blinking in slow recovery.
How can anything that size occur without warning?
If I ever teach piano again
I'll use you to demonstrate sforzando.

I can predict the ones in the car
and grab the wheel in time to save us.
You always sneeze when we drive past the morgue.
Is this how you explode the lie of death?
Or is it in memory of your mother,
a fatalist who never a blessed a sneezer,
but always said, with great solemnity,
that one is never closer to death
than when sneezing?

Your mother never knew your daughter
who unknowingly inherited her sneezes—
short bursts, always occurring in odd numbers—
khew, khew, khew, khew, khew,
like a child I once knew who made that sound
whenever he shot someone with his toy gun.
I still bless her too when her granddaughter sneezes.

On Finding Yet Another Fineliner Pen in the Bottom of the Washing Machine, After the Load Has Been Removed

The poet's wife remembers her foolish refusal
to check anyone else's pockets. It's a privacy thing,
she claims, like reading someone's mail.
It's really the unsayable fear of what might be found.
But now, she plucks it up, wondering
with one half of her brain how tightly
the cap is sealed, with the other half
adding up the cost of several pair
of cream-colored chinos she's just stuffed
into the dryer.

And now she removes its chewed lid
with mindless concentration, like Mark Twain
as he opened one of his wife's letters,
"By mistake. To see what was inside."
Abundance of the pure black
spills over her hands, indelible.
They tremble under the weight
of all the unwritten poems flowing
into her fingers, causing them to print.
Wordless.

And now she's opened that chewed lid
to discover a well of black ink
that flows over her fingers, etching their prints,
onto the white enamel of the machines,
falling in larger circles on a creamy marble counter,
falling finally onto the brown quarry tile floor
in monochromatic wastage
like seed on barren surfaces.

She cleans the machine, the counter, the floor
but her left little finger is still stained.
She doesn't know if it's a mark left
to remind her of her dereliction of duty,
her folly of curiosity about the unborn
poems in that vial of fluid,
or a baptism into his world
where words are flesh.
Finally she takes a laundry marker
and writes her own poem on a paper bag:

Housewife Haiku

The poet's best pen
falls into his wife's washtub
Black plus white makes grey.

For I Shall Consider My Beloved

I can read writin', but I can't write readin'.
    Sis' Rabbit

who writes with the left hand but is never gauche
who writes with the left hand because
it is the most direct path from heart to paper.
His keyboard also has eighty-eight keys,
like my piano. I manage those keys
with much more ease perhaps
because they too are unlettered
But the pen in the hand is as direct
as two hands poised above any keyboard.

The machined hand is unknown until sign-off.
Reader cannot know writer, can take no notice
of the loops and curls that sculpt the I of Me.
I want to wrap these vowels for you
in silken consonants, opulent, dignified,
asserted by a fountain pen.

Moons

Half-Moon

a half-circle half framed
by a corner of window
The sky descends into ultramarine,
its pale belly tickled by a line of spruce
made black by the coming dark.
The bare elm, every twig puffed up
with hoar-frosted importance,
protests every degree of daylight fading.
I must go tell the rabbits to prepare for gazing

Double Moons

The moon is full tonight
swollen, impaled on a naked branch of elm
Seen through the double-glazed window
it has a shadow moon
caught on the same branch
but much paler than its living twin
A phantom flattened into the wall
of the womb we call the sky.

All of It

The moon came to full—
protean celestial manjou—
crosshatched by window screen.
I waited for the whole round cake,
thought it would never be mine.

Then, one afternoon, walking with you
over plangent wet leaves,
our moon lay on the horizon
horizontal, overstuffed,
familiar as cheese.

The Lucky Ones

Looking over the intent heads
all bent to catch the softest voice in the class
Outside an early Spring evening gilds the city
with a single-malt light
beneath a cover of snow-laden cloud
As they reach down into their metaphor packs
I stop the class. Call attention to it—

snow

See it from cloud's eye view
Let fall the oafish gangs
impeded by their collective weight
Then watch the lucky ones catch fire
as they enter the streetlight's orbit
spiral down in final glorious jag
taking with them
our collective breath
single-malt light

Binaries

Two of our friends have discovered each other
their new combined radiance far exceeds
both the light and the warmth we cherish them for.
I sit over lunch with them, noticing
how she praises the couscous of his old country,
how he succumbs to Baskin and Robbins,
bringing their circles into sweet congruity.
She's trying to make him a Trekkie.
He's more than willing.
He tells us he's never watched the show,
"but there are some lines I know very well:
Zip me up, Scotty." I say goodbye.
I'll record every episode for them.
The summer sun beams down.

"The Most Recent 5000 Years of Chinese Art"

I WEST MEETS EAST

I take the elevator up, to begin at the top,
at the end of the long spiral
that winds up the tunnel of Wright's inverted mountain.
Mistake. I hit the middle and come face to face
with a 2500-year-old head—a bronze head
whose eyes scrutinize me
from caves beneath hooded lids.
We stand, locked in each other's gaze—
the moving meets the unmoved mover.

II Wu Wei

"Nothing can please many, and please long, but just representations of general nature."
    Dr. Johnson

There's something to be said for a culture
that takes the long view. Few eccentrics
or eccentricities survive. But
Wu Wei still causes a scandal
500 years after his death:
He painted fishermen in furry vests
hauling nets in to the shore. Got himself
expelled from court repeatedly, and
repeatedly called back. His drunkenness
was tolerated only because of his inspiration.
The seasmell still rises off his canvas,
and I can smell the wet fur.

III Northern Song Dynasty Leopards

The snow leopards
once ornately fierce
have danced off all their spots
slipped into background
and hide now in the underglaze
of the brown ceramic jar.

IV Tan Tea Box

Old dark wood, strapped with gold and silver
a cage, really. Two gilded birds are perched on top.
I watch them closely; they might fly away.

V Han Horse

Small enough to fit the hand
if its wings were folded
but it crouches, ready
for two thousand years
still poised, waiting
for this great spring.

VI Spiral

At the top of the circular climb
rests the ultimate Bodhisattva
a life-sized sandstone head
Large pendulous ears—
his sculptor knew the way of old men's ears—
they just keep growing—
the smooth-lidded eyes end
in lines of equanimity
parallel to the horizon
the fixed stone orbs
see past the human gaze
into infinite infinities
the lips put to shame
da Vinci's pet enigma
This is god/head
transcendental, still looking
despite a slightly damaged nose—
as if blossoms of Spring's first plums
have just opened the fine nostrils
after a millennium of interment
in the Wanfo Temple garden

Mosaic Tiles, Bathing Room, Fishbourne Roman Palace

The boy, careless as only
a boy can be
straddles the carefree dolphin
They ride the mosaic floor
that rippled for a hundred years
beneath unsandalled Roman bathers

The clay beneath them has heaved
century-slow, giving more of a curve
to the dolphin's undulating back
and a slippage into grin
on their two forever faces.
We walk the warmed mosaic,
our soles tickled by their rippling smiles

"Ovid's Love Nest Found by Banks of The Tiber"

—Sunday Times

Under three meters of clay, walls
and an in-floor mosaic, of Dionysus, perhaps?
White-flecked beard and laurel crown,
carrying a flowering, beribboned staff.
"It could be an ideal poet, perhaps Greek.
But we prefer to think it is Ovid."

The villa overlooks the Tiber from the North
and from its portico the poet might have watched
the traffic stream over a bridge and on up the Milvian Way.
But I imagine him turning back, over the threshold
into the cool columned retreat from a city so embroiled
that the four red walls offered serenity.

Old Master of the Ars Amatoria, keep your silence.
The truth about Livia could lead a historian to suspect
that you were banished for refusing your emperor's wife
not for joining the traffic that streamed
so steadily through his daughter's bedroom.
Your words, despite the centuries of clay
that have clogged that porticoed retreat,
still sigh to lovers, as lovers sigh to them.

Elgin Marbles, British Museum

The horses' heads are raised above
imagination's surface
Hooves thrash, lunging through
the airy Attic stone. Fear of drowning
into this present flares their nostrils
leaps in their cold wide eyes.
The horsemen recede into the stone
reclaimed into chaste marble
their cries of battle stilled, mute
to the bold barbarian stares,
the coarse paws that have rubbed
their perfect muscular curves
to a vulgar Saxon shine.

Docent Muse

For My Daughter

You revel in the Renaissance
sing along with Palestrina—
always the first alto line—
crave your own viola d'amore.

You showed me a current favorite,
a Renaissance Annunciation,
your arm moving in a rising arc
of unconscious grace, a precise answer
to Gabriel's downward arching wing
I felt the feathered breeze of both—
ekphrasis
ekstasis

Ave Maria, gratia plena	The Virgin sits in a high-ceilinged, airy chamber.
You were always looking	She's always reading. Anachronism of the book,
at the pictures, reading	a St. Joseph's Daily Missal, the page open
every available book	to the picture of herself, seated, in the same room reading the same book, ad infinitum.
Dominus tecum	Rote-learned Latin brooks no hesitation. She is in the company of lilies. This was the truest beatitude.

You planted lilies in the garden beneath your window
    The small museum copy of the Winged Victory
      still awaits your return, its wings in stasis.

Benedicta tu in mulieribus   "Blessed art thou among women,"
                                     that wasn't saying a great deal,
                                     all things considered.
May you be blessed
among daughters,

et Benedictus fructus ventris   "And blessed is the fruit of
    tui Jesus.   thy womb, Jesus."
                                   And then, the intake of her startled
                                          breath—
                                   the angel gone, no chance,
                                        no need to question.
                                   The scent of the lilies intensified,
                                   stirred by Gabriel's wings.

In your room I've placed lilies on your desk
    where I too, read, and await
        the miracle sent from angel lip to virgin ear
            received from the airborne scent
                the sweet seminal drop pending
                      from the stamen, never falling,
                          there's miracle enough in that.

Sancta Maria, Mater Dei   How sudden the transformation
                                   from virgin to matron to queen,
                                   the interim servitude
                                   uncounted and still
                                   Mother is subservient to Son:
ora pro nobis peccatoribus   "Pray for us sinners," indeed
nunc et in hora mortis nostrae. "Now and at the hour of our
                                         death."

Amen. But what of those interim hours, months, years?

And then the Child says to her: "Dost not thou know
 that I must be about my Father's business?"
  A question no daughter ever asks, knowing
   we all must be about our mothers' business
    without ever being told what that business is,
     just casually betrayed into it by
      silent example.

So fly, my Muse-Child, wise in the ways of the word
 if not the ways of the world. Be your own
  Winged Victory, your own annunciating angel.
   Fiat.

III
Tiger Side of Night

Icons

I ELEKTRA

I am the icon of filial piety
(to the wrong parent)
spared my sister's fate
by nothing more than a breeze.
But we've been taught to believe
that the first sin is never the father's.
Is it that easy to accept the sacrifice
of a virgin daughter, a sweet sister,
to save a wife who, after all,
may have left of her own free will?
Before they embarked in their thousand ships
did anyone think to write Auntie Helen
and ask her how things were across that water?

II Antigone

I was always the good one, the pleading one
the damned fool
Did I really imagine my brother
would have done for me
what I tried to do for him?

III Clytaemnestra

More sinned against—
I dare any of you who have mothered a daughter,
I dare your blame. And then,
After ten years without a word,
the only surprise is that I took to bed
only one lover. How many times
did he betray me?
And then there was the matter of Cassandra—
That chick had some mouth on her
when she was riled.
Thank the gods nobody listened.

IV Cassandra

The sailors called me sullen
Krypsynos, a word of one use—
to describe the mind of a woman—
"closed and secretive as the crypt"
and for nothing else.
I stood in the cart all the way to Mycenae.
It seemed less of an acquiescence.
The old man felt obliged to stand too
lest I see his baldness.

I saw everything. I see everything.
I can tell you now how little it will get you,
silenced by disbelief.
Silent. But seeing. Waiting.

V Helen

What is it you want to know?
Did I go willingly?
Does it matter now, after all the blood?
Your brother-kings all looked at me,
with lust more foul than the stranger's.
And Paris, you must admit, was a good deal younger,
more handsome, and offered the chance to travel.
But most of all, he desired me
not to make other men envious,
but for his pleasure, and mine.

VI Iphigenia

Lexi, Orestes, Daddy says I'm going to be married today!
I can't wait to see my husband!
I wonder which prince Daddy's picked for me?
I hope he's not too old and serious.
Everybody around here is so glum these days,
waiting for the wind to blow.

Oh, Mommy, such a beautiful dress,
such flowers! Such jewels! All for me?
Mommy, why are you crying?

Cleopatra, the Final Sting

It wasn't kneeling to young Octavius
or having to clasp the worm of Nilus,
It wasn't outliving her Antony.
It wasn't even the threat of saucy lictors
nor of being "squeaked" by a boy.

It is being written about by first-year students:
the foul-complexioned clods who berate her
for being the consummate manipulator,
scorning Antony's choice of love over power,
(She'd have had them whipped
for their aesthetic offences alone)
the prissy teen sorority girls
(they could take a papyrus or two from her scroll)
shocked at a queen who knew
both lust and love
and had the wit to enjoy both.

Ironing

So much of what we prize is formed by heat and intense pressure: the awful power of a volcano, the sparkle of diamonds, the feel of well-pressed clothing.

Retreat from the swirling wringing action
of a household I no longer control
to the ironing board, my friend
that has its arthritic squeaks too.
The spray bottle has fluid in its lungs.
Only the iron is healthy, a small determined dragon
creating that addictive scent of steaming hot cotton.

All these comfort me
as I press order, smoothness, knife-pleats
onto basketfuls of wrinkled chaos.
There is a certain piety attendant on this act
It has become less a chore than a ritual
making the crooked straight, the rough places plain
I am the high priestess of Smooth.

I press the tablecloths and memories rise
with the pure perfume of steamed hot linen,
the tinctures of conversations remaining
though all the wine stains have disappeared.

Cleaning Windows

This is one task guaranteed reassuringly futile
constantly required
Window: a feminine symbol
because it lets in light
lets out the staled airs of living
is transparent, clear and frangible
every speck of dirt shows, and
only breakage is forever.

Blue and White

> *I could decorate a whole house in blue and white,*
> *but I'd have to change my life to live in it.*
> Anonymous Woman

On the way back from dinner, I linger
in front of a china shop called "Blue and White."
The ware ranges from Ming to Spode,
to mysterious Staffordshire "flo blue."
I am drawn into the rooms I imagine
around each plate, ewer and basin.
In such rooms hang the scents of jasmine
of lavender, iris, and white rose.
In such rooms, voices are always low, musical.
Viols and theorboes are played.
Questions are only either/or.
In such rooms, no one ever dies.
But in such rooms, one could.

The Comfort of Lists

She keeps at least one in every room
to hold exhaustion at bay—
tries not to sit down until every task is crossed off.
Lists must be consulted. They are proof
of need, of connection to the world
if only through the tenuousness of the vacuum hose,
floors scrubbed, windows cleaned, inside and out—
she remembered one Christmas Day
it was warm enough to do the outside windows
without the ammonia freezing in the squeejee
It was, she thought, her best Christmas ever.

Each New Year's Eve she contrived to be
scrubbing the kitchen floor at midnight
on the principle that whatever you are doing then
you will do a lot throughout the coming year.

She tries to keep the deepfreeze filled—
on a rotating basis of course—
with enough baked goods for her wake.
And there's an envelope with cash enough
for her favourite malt to serve the mourners—
God knows who'll clean up afterwards.

Laryngitis

I am infolding
a form inviolable
no seams visible
no cord
attaches me
to anything

My ears have begun job retraining
Glenn Gould's muttering hum
has become the fifth voice of a fugue
a reasonable presumption of God's will

My vision is sharpening, colors intensifying
and I'm learning to read lips,
feel the sensuality of muscles
that surround other mouths.

I imagine myself talking—
but hear with the inmost ear
only my own stale inconsequence, see
with the inner eye such futile workings
of my own fever-parched lips.

Who could not anticipate
what might be spoken, or why?
Better to let God write his own fugues
than to mutter out my monotone.

I've been silent for a week—
but am considering something
of much longer duration.

I read of a man who is silent on Sundays.
Does he call it a fast, a retreat,
a vacation?
Will this absence of calling
become a vocation?

Radius

The slight thinning of the upper limb before
decision of knot and twigs

The place where eye and skeleton first meet
to argue over the lumpen end of adolescent radius

The embarrassment of a growth spurt
that thrusts beyond the sleeve's end

The friction of one bone moving around its rigid sibling
the envy of staid ulna for kinetic radius

Veins, arteries contending in the carpal tunnel
frighten the nearby nerves into shakes or paralysis

The skin of the forearm, speckled, freckled,
a transitional texture between work-hardened hands
and smooth upper arm

All in all, anatomy not worth anatomizing

Until

You took my hand in both of yours
turned it palm-side up
kissed the inside of my wrist
and felt my pulse racing toward your lips.

Failing the Eye Exam

"I'm going to examine your inner eye."

The drops have given me brown-eyed susans
visible in the mirror before all
vision fades, and blinded, I navigate
by sound, direction of his nervous breath
intermittent on my saffron-stained cheek
in a clinical intimacy that discomfits us both.

"Try to look straight ahead
don't look into the light"
 (I see blood vessels spreading
like cracks in a newly-formed desert—
a whole coppery field of non-vision)

From a polished surface of the machine
the skin around my eyes is reflected
a glowing turquoise pattern of fine lines.
But there is a bright yellow comet streaking toward my nose.
Should I tell the resident
or allow him the frisson of discovery?

When a doctor says, "This is interesting,"
it's like when the tests come back "positive;"
you know it's nothing of the sort.

Bone Scan

Do bones scan like poetry,
long-lined angular rhythms singing,
gamma particles dancing
for an unknown radiologist
who might report that my bones
have taken up the phosphates
with warm, excited attraction?
Is this the ultimate introspection?

The technician says lie still, relax.
But I tingle all over knowing
this flawed poem is my body
this flawed body is my poem
formed in my dark unknowing,
read randomly, out of sequence—
and, as my wee daughter declared,
"a picture with the skin tooken off."
Is a poem, then, below the words,
beyond mere sensation
unknown, born in the crimson marrow?

Breaking Through

It was pain that made the world.

On this day the pain explained itself.
The wines were perfect with that dinner.
This was the evening the gardenia bloomed. Double.
The chamber music was all Russian.
The moon on the drive home was a saffron oval
overlaid with indigo clouds.

The carnations on the desk remain perfect.
The pain still throbs
but tonight it's in perfect time
to a particularly drunken fugue of Shostakovitch.
Dmitry, you knew the pain of betrayal
you wrote through the pain
you wrote because of the pain.

The Widower

The whole word an inarticulate "without her."
The long "i" shortened to a hiccup
brought on by his sobbing
and by his attempts not to sob.
The sound more hollow than "widow."
He would not use the word himself.

Together since Grade Four, they competed
for the best grades, the athletic prizes,
the wittiest remarks.

Now the spur is gone,
the "old horse" (their words for each other)
longs only for the finish line.

Sub-Titled

Someday
she will learn to swallow praise with grace
without chewing
to find the hidden bones of criticism.

She will learn to look in mirrors
without blushing
at her own presumption.

She will not hold a hand
in front of her mouth
when she speaks in company.

She will speak, unasked, of desire.
Someday.

The Tiger Side of Night

for Willy Vogelzang

Midsummer midnight in the parking lot
The most mundane task evokes
the most surprising responses
memories of midsummernights past—
meeting my neighbor over garbage taking-out
watching the aurora borealis
collecting night cats

Tonight I wish her back in life
for the pleasure she would find
in the friendly Burman who walks with me
along the top of the low posts.
He walks on my tiger side,
slightly behind me, and at the perfect height.
Together we cast shadows that render us
Neanderthal woman, saber-toothed kitten
against suburban garage doors.
We could prowl like this until dawn.

For Dodie

You always hated the month of March.
Its muddiness, its winds were a personal affront.
And you were such a force of nature
we all expected the month to be cancelled.
And now we are gathered, prepared
to hate all Marches forever, for you,
stolen from us by this month of mad winds.

You told me once your favourite season was Autumn,
when you appeared, like Demeter, sharing your bounty
of pickles, chutneys, and Chinese lanterns
that you always claimed "just grew."
We knew better, Dodie: they wouldn't
have dared do otherwise for you.

A friend for all months, all seasons,
you live in memory, timeless,
steadfast as the pink bleeding-heart you kept by your front door,
indomitable as the marigolds that lined your front walk,
an honor guard as upright as your own imperial form.

And now, Good Lady, take your rest.
Disport yourself with the other goddesses,
but do be patient with them. It will take time
for them to learn your virtue, your decorum.

Stones

Lapidary

Polish stones picked up from dry stream beds.
But first, soften each one in the mouth.
Learn the taste of granite, take pumice
as your salad. For dessert
there will be fresh opals,
the precious gem of ill luck.
Those you must swallow whole.
The only cure is to let stones
 replace your inner organs.

Agate

Syllables, not surface
landscape turned on its side
revealing strata of warm deserts,
without sandstorms
without snakes.

Beryl

A name for a woman of a certain age
cabochon-cut, hard, but easy
to see through.

BLOODSTONE

When I learned the lore
my birthstone was "the bloodstone."
A conjuring of opposites
I became a paradox to myself:
"You can't get blood out of a stone."
I knew it had something to do with stinginess
so I wasn't altogether surprised at the spanking I got
for selfishness, having taken a whole stick of gum.
So I've avoided that stone with its unexpected clots of red
confined in, betrayed by, a murky green.
And for me, most meanings of blood
have been washed away.

CHRYSOCHOLLA

This whole planet seen from near space
wide cerulean lapping at tropical green.
The miniature planets lie cushioned
in a velvet-lined casket
too beautiful to wear
too beautiful not to wear.

DIAMONDS

Always best in the plural.

JADE

The spirit in the jade is the divine bear
strong stone to contain strong spirit.
The Hong-shan ground black-bear jade
into blades long enough to find the heart.
I feel the cold shaft going through fur
hear my jadespirit roar out into the chill air.

LIANZHU JADE

Lianzhu jade gets brighter with age.
The leisure of the atelier hums in every line.
No matter if the father dies before
the slender tube is hollowed—
the son, or the grandson, will finish.

LAPIS LAZULI

Opaque as long-term pain,
doesn't bear looking into
only semi-precious
a spectacular bruise
hardened into emblem
that's why they call the blues the blues

QUARTZ

The eye of a certain beetle is made up of some twenty thousand
quartz crystals.
A perfect marriage of animal and mineral. No vegetables need apply.

RUTILATED QUARTZ

Impurities bedded in the purest clarity
a bundle of thin golden needles
aligned, a standing army
entrapped, at attention
for eternity.

Hematite

My pre-teen year and all I wanted in the whole world
was a "black diamond" ring. It broke into pieces
when I tried to test its hardness. With a hammer.

My brother the psychopath gave a 'black diamond'
to the girl he persuaded to marry him, telling her
it was more precious than the white kind.
She believed it, so it seemed fit enough.
I was compelled to play the organ for their wedding.
I played the Dead March from *Saul*.

Obsidian

Very Black. Very polished. Very Sharp.
A perfect natural glass.
A perfect natural knife.
My favourite Sicilian Donna
has a ring fashioned in a flower-shape
from some of Aetna's finest.

Labradorite

I keep a large chunk named identity.
Its surfaces have been machined, polished
to reveal the multi-hued light beneath.
True brilliance is always there,
just beyond my reach.
Mostly, I'm grateful to see it, hold it
without demanding its secrets.

DIAMOND REPRISE

A chemist I knew once made the claim
that "diamonds are chemically boring.
Just pure carbon." And so, I decided,
was he, despite his chemical complexity.

BOULDER OPAL

Deep B minor blue shot through
with surprise of brilliant parrot-green.
One tradition calls it the stone of ill luck
but I'll take my chances with it.

Hampstead

I IN MEMORIAM MAGGIE WILLIAMSON

The walk from the tube stop to Keats's house
takes us past Maggie's Corner—officially named
after the woman who sold flowers there
for sixty years without missing a day.
The blue plaque on the wall gives no details
such as which sixty, or which sixty of her years
But her steadfastness, which would have moved Keats,
has inspired someone to open a shop
on the same site, but inside the building.
We buy jasmine from one ghost
to take to another.

II The House

It's fenced off, hedged, protected
as we'd want his house to be.
The front walk is bordered with old rosemary
that releases its scent to my passing skirt.
The door is closed, but not locked.

Inside the rooms are small and many:
writers need compartments.
We gaze in silence on his relics—
souvenirs of him and his "fair creature of an hour"
then walk up stairs to the poet's bedroom
I do and do not want to see it—

His bed is a tiny curtained bower,
all the bedclothes are heavy white cotton.
Across the white counterpane a large white towel
is draped, and at its centre,
a small round indentation.
A discreet note on a nearby wall explains:
the towel is there for Beauty,
who found her own way into the house, the bed,
and the housekeepers' good graces.
Later, we will find Beauty herself
in the small shop in the basement,
asleep in a box near the shopkeeper
who tells us, "She never complains
or meows, even if we're late with her dinner."

III Memento

We leave with postcards and a book, weeping
for love unconsummate, genius unfruited.
The tears from Fancy's eye have polished
the glass between the poet and his urn,
and we who love now see its chill reflection
more clearly than the urn itself.
We want and do not want
to break that glass.

IV THE GARDEN

Back outside, a fine mist hovers.
A blackbird sings unseen in the tall hedge,
and though all the flowers are proclaiming May
a slight autumnal shiver shadows us.
We hold hands tightly all the way home.

Red Rose, White Rose

TOWTON FIELD

I still pick up stones wherever I go.
That reddish boulder quite deceived me.
I picked it up for its colour—faded bloodstain.
The topside was so smooth it looked worked.
Its other side looks almost new-formed
as if those thickly spaced holes were made
by hard rain on dry sand
or blood falling hard on everything
in the heat of those three days
when the world they knew turned to blood and fire
and the only way out was back down the hill
and into the fast-freezing waters—
waters that would run red at Spring thaw.

It lies atop a hill, a cornfield now
its only monument a modest stone obelisk
with the date, 1461, carved
on its sturdy base. Someone has left
two wreaths intertwined—red roses and white—
red blood white snow

Even on a warm May afternoon
the wind up here is constant and chill
and clouds appear from nowhere
to excoriate with Palm Sunday memories.

Balancing Act

Psyche, disguised as an azure phoenix,
crashes through Reason's skylight
to break its neck on the blue
square of a Mondrian geometric.

After the hailstorm, the heavens brightening,
the scent of ozone purifying the air
and the sun's apology carried
from the west on a warming breeze
a plausible critique of pure reason,
and the best we can hope for

unless

the painter's unfrenzied eye
finding the perspective point
where reason and illusion meet
distills for all time the dance
of jeweled desire
and nature's reasoned minuet.

Fugue State

We maintain this fragile balance
while singing toward Armageddon:
first voice unknown
entries all too early to remember
who began that theme.
The subjects never change except
to grow louder, or diminish,
and sometimes there is an exposed solo—yes,
we recognize that protracted howl of the fanatic
that frightened liberal yip
the steady rhythmic barking of the dogs of war
the well-tempered lamentations of the peace-lovers.
But the dog we call the past keeps bounding up
always on our blind side
grabs an arm in his canines
to stop us mid-reach of a future.

What You Will Need

Take with you to the high caves a sharp stylus
to carve your story into the walls.
Take goats, geese, and a horse
for vellum, quill, and bow-hair.
At night you will creep down
stiff with mountain cold
to take resin from tree-line pines.
And remember—an obsidian shard
sharp enough to draw blood
for when the ink fails.
You will crave music enough
to skin a wildcat and stretch the gut carefully
alongside the hide. You will be grateful
for the perfect proportion of twisted
entrails to the length of your arm.
Venture further down the mountain
to find spruce for the body
of the instrument you will play
to charm the new neighbors to your fires.

Pazyryk Fragment

Men on reindeer gentle as carousel ponies
nose-to-tail in mock-solemn cocksure procession
around the square now re-woven and lying
tamely on the living room floor

They call to mind the Ellesmere Manuscript—
The Canterbury Tales—with the fat poet
on a horse not big enough to carry him
on any pilgrimage beyond the innyard.
They too have over-large heads, pointed beards, tasseled hats.
It's those reindeer that make them strange, that seem
so reconciled to their saddles and the weight they bear,
their riders' feet almost grazing the ground.
Their reins are slackened—no fear of them bolting.

I cannot find the flaw said to be woven
into every carpet, like a signature.
Nor can I solve the riddle of how
the original rug fetched up in a cave in Siberia
frozen in fresh water for a thousand years.
Were its weavers exiled from their Persian homes?
Were reindeer ridden in—or into—their empire?

The latest shipment of carpets from Iran
includes some tribal wools from Hamadan
with grey helicopters, dark red guns
and bright yellow bombs in a khaki field
inside a traditional geometric border.
If you look closely, you can see verse woven in:
words from the Koran—a prayer for peace.

Acknowledgments

Some of these poems have appeared in:

Alberta Views ("My Sister's Hands")
Amethyst Review ("Elgin Marbles")
Ariel ("Lampblack")
The Fiddlehead ("Balance of Nature," "Gesundheit," "Mallow," "A Little World Made Cunningly," "Hand Poems")
Room of One's Own ("A Sketch of the Old Man")
The Windhover ("Deconsecrations")
"Bone Scan" appeared on the *Edmonton Stroll of Poets* website. "A Sketch of the Old Man" was also published as a broadside by the Huckleberry Press (Big Arm, Montana, 1992)
"Red Rose, White Rose," "Balancing Act" "What You Will Need," "Fugue State" and "Pazyryk Fragment" won the CBC Alberta Anthology 2003 competition under the collective title, "Singing Toward Armageddon."
"My Sister's Hands" won second prize in the Petra Kenney Memorial Competition, and "On Finding Another Pilot Fineliner" won third prize in the Stephen Leacock Competition.
Other poems have been performed on the CBC's radio program, *Alberta Anthology*.
"Tarpits" appeared in *Standing Together*, an anthology published by Brindle and Glass.

This book was written with the generous support of grants from the Alberta Foundation for the Arts and the Canada Council.

I would also like to thank the following people for their careful reading and comments on my work: Bert Almon, Meli Costopoulos, Vasilis Costopoulos, Shawna Lemay, Lee Elliott, Michael Penny, Kimmy Beach, and Iman Mersal. Thanks go also to Michael McCarthy and to Les Murray, soul brother.